Advance praise

"Prayer is one of the most powerful weapons available to the believer.

If you choose to read this book, you are choosing to enter a wonderful and mysterious place.

If you choose to apply and practice its contents, you will be freed to pray in new and dynamic ways.

In the years that Sandra Schroeder was in my church, she inspired me with her devotion, discipline, and the example of someone who was clearly a seasoned veteran of prayer. The Bible says in Daniel 11:32, "The people who know their God shall be strong, and carry out great exploits" (NKJV). Sandra certainly has proven that she knows God intimately. Her prayer life has born much fruit. I am sure this book will be a valuable volume, in encouraging both the parent and the child in helping to seek a greater grasp of the architecture, mystery, and adventures of prayer."

—Paul Berteig
Senior Pastor, Timbers Community Church
Prince George, B.C.

"Prayer is a vital part of the life of a Christian and as Christian parents, it is essential that we teach our children to pray. *100 Prayers for Children* is a great tool to help any parent who wants to disciple their kids in this area. Linking Scripture with the prayers for each day provides an all-in-one source for helping your child learn to walk with God. Get this book...and get your kids praying! God bless!"

—Doug Phaneuf
Pastor, Living Springs Christian Fellowship
Airdrie, Alberta

100 PRAYERS FOR CHILDREN

Sandra Schroeder

Pray Always!
Sandra

100 PRAYERS FOR CHILDREN
Copyright © 2017 by Sandra Schroeder

Scripture quotations marked "ESV" are from The Holy Bible, English Standard Version® (ESV®), copyright © 2001 by Crossway, a publishing ministry of Good News Publishers. Used by permission. All rights reserved. Scripture marked "NASB" taken from the New American Standard Bible®, Copyright © 1960, 1962, 1963, 1968, 1971, 1972, 1973, 1975, 1977, 1995 by The Lockman Foundation. Used by permission. Scripture marked "NIV" taken from the Holy Bible, NEW INTERNATIONAL VERSION®. Copyright © 1973, 1978, 1984, 2011 by Biblica, Inc. All rights reserved worldwide. Used by permission. NEW INTERNATIONAL VERSION® and NIV® are registered trademarks of Biblica, Inc. Use of either trademark for the offering of goods or services requires the prior written consent of Biblica US, Inc. Scripture marked "NKJV" taken from the New King James Version®. Copyright © 1982 by Thomas Nelson, Inc. Used by permission. All rights reserved.

Printed in Canada

ISBN: 978-1-4866-1436-3

Word Alive Press
131 Cordite Road, Winnipeg, MB R3W 1S1
www.wordalivepress.ca

Library and Archives Canada Cataloguing in Publication

Schroeder, Sandra, author
    100 prayers for children / Sandra Schroeder.

Issued in print and electronic formats.
ISBN 978-1-4866-1436-3 (softcover).--ISBN 978-1-4866-1437-0 (ebook)

    1. Children--Prayers and devotions. 2. Prayers--Juvenile literature.
I. Title. II. Title: One hundred prayers for children.

BV265.S37 2017   j242'.82   C2017-901476-5
                                          C2017-901477-3

This book was given to:

_____

From

_____

Message

_____

_____

_____

_____

CONTENTS

(On how, who and what to pray for)

AUTHOR'S DEDICATION

I would like to dedicate this book to my seven wonderful grandchildren, whom I love and cherish very much. I pass on to you how I learned to pray in faith using God's Word, the Bible. My Lord and Saviour has never, ever let me down. Put your trust in Him and He will do the same for you.

Thank you to my dear husband who has trusted in me, giving me space and a time of peace for me to focus on writing.

Thank you to my two sons and daughters-in-law for the joy, awesome inspiration and spice of life that they have brought to our home.

In memory of both my parents for their steadfast Christian upbringing and for the examples they set in their faithfulness to God. They trusted and believed in God for their whole lives. Even in times of difficulty and hardship, they trusted in God for deliverance and were not disappointed. They had a strong hope in the Lord.

Most importantly, I wish to dedicate these prayers back to the Lord Jesus Christ, my true, dear and faithful friend. His Spirit has inspired me and guided me to pray from the heart. He has created in me the desire to share in this book on how God's Word has taught me to pray.

FOREWORD

It is simultaneously humbling and rewarding for me to realize that God has used me to birth something significant through my itinerant ministry of over four decades. Periodically, I am made aware of how the Holy Spirit has brought forth some lasting fruit and generated multiple blessings to others. God has inspired an obedient follower of Jesus or a group of them to take the risk of believing God and addressing a challenge or meeting a need.

Sandra Schroeder was stirred by the Holy Spirit to create two helpful items through two separate prayer seminars that I taught in two different locations. First, in Prince George, British Columbia after my *Prayer Dynamics Seminar* she was prompted to produce "Prayer Cards" which proved effective for many. Second, during the *Unleashing Intercession Seminar* in Airdrie, Alberta, Sandra was led to create *100 PRAYERS FOR CHILDREN,* which I believe is a tool the Lord will mightily use.

God wants each of us to grow in the discipline of prayer. This is why our Lord Jesus readily responded with the Lord's Prayer when His disciples requested Him to teach them to pray (Matthew

6:9-13; Luke 11:1-4). If the disciples of Jesus needed to learn to pray, we also need to learn to pray. What better time to begin that journey of learning than when we are children?

I trust Sandra's book will motivate Christian parents and grandparents to help their children and grandchildren begin the journey of prayer.

—Dr. T.V. Thomas, Ex. 3:14
Director, Centre for Evangelism
& World Mission

A NOTE FROM SANDRA ABOUT THE BOOK

This is a prayer and devotional book suitable for children ages eight and up.

The book should be used together with the parents or grandparents.

The child can also use the book by themselves when they are able to understand how to apply the devotions and learn by themselves to pray.

First read the devotional scripture and think about it.

Second, learn to pray the prayer sample and apply it to the child's personal life.

Thirdly, memorize the scripture verse.

In this book are several prayer phrases that I learned as a child.

I have written this book to encourage parents to help their child to learn how to pray. I have also given some scripture meditations for them to think about.

May the child find that greater adventure with God in having their prayers answered as they come into an honest relationship with Jesus Christ.

—Sandra

HOW TO PRAY FROM YOUR HEART

- God has made a way for you to talk to Him. This is called prayer.
- You can talk to Him quietly in your mind or you can talk out loud. God wants you to talk to Him often. *"Call to me and I will answer you..."*(Jeremiah 33:3, NIV)
- Pray sincerely from your heart with your feelings and emotions, whether you are joyful or thankful, or even if you are sad and want to cry.
- Just tell God exactly how it is. You can even ask for His help.
- God understands everything you say and how you feel about it. You can talk to God about anything, whenever you want to. Use your own thoughts or words.
- The prayers in this book are samples to guide you in how you can pray.

READ AND THINK ABOUT
JOHN 21:4-14

God, You are so good all the time;
Your love is so great and amazing.
We thank You
for this food to enjoy.
Amen!

Memory Verse: *"Have faith in God."*
(Mark 11:22, ESV)

READ AND THINK ABOUT
JOHN 6:26-35

Dear Lord Jesus, thank You for this very special
birthday for _____, the one we love so dear.
Give to _____ a very special year, with many
adventures and new opportunities to take.
Thank You for the food and for
the delicious birthday cake.
Bless our fun time of celebration. Amen!

Memory Verse: *"I am the living bread
that came down from heaven."*
(John 6:51, ESV)

READ AND THINK ABOUT

1 KINGS 17:1-16

Dear Lord Jesus, thank You for this food
and for this time together.
Thank You for Your presence as our guest.
May this food to us be blessed. Amen!

Memory Verse: *"...God is love."*
(1 John 4:8, ESV)

READ AND THINK ABOUT
MATTHEW 15:32-38

Dear Lord Jesus, thank You for this good food
and even the healthy vegetables too. Help me
to eat a little of everything. We ask You now
to bless it and to nourish our bodies to good
health. Bless the conversation that we
lovingly share with one another.
Thank You for this time as we bow to
You in prayer. Amen!

Memory Verse: *"I am the bread of life."*
(John 6:48, ESV)

READ AND THINK ABOUT
MARK 8:1-9

Dear Lord Jesus, please come to our table and dine with us. We cherish every moment with You. Thanks for plenty of food for all of us. You satisfy our hungry hearts, body and soul. As we share this meal with family, please keep us, bind us together and make us whole. Amen!

Memory Verse: *"He has brought me to his banquet hall, and his banner over me is love."* (Song of Solomon 2:4, NASB)

READ AND THINK ABOUT
MARK 6:33-44

Dear Lord Jesus, thank You for listening as
we pray. I know Your answer is already on
the way. Thank You for the food we have
for each and every day. For any wrong we
may have done this day, we ask You
to please forgive and erase.
Come now and surround us with
Your love and saving grace. Amen!

Memory Verse: *"Oh give thanks to
the Lord; call upon his name."*
(Psalm 105:1, ESV)

READ AND THINK ABOUT
2 KINGS 4:8-17

Dear God, thank You for the beauty of the world. You made it all so wonderfully complete and sweet. Come now and bless this food You have given us to eat. Amen!

Memory Verse: *"Oh, taste and see that the Lord is good!"*
(Psalm 34:8, ESV)

MATTHEW 25:31-40

Dear God, thank You for food and drink, and for the wonderful thoughts of me that You think. Of all the good You bring each day, I thank You God for Your true love today. Amen!

Memory Verse: *"Love your neighbour as yourself."*
(Matthew 22:39, NIV)

READ AND THINK ABOUT
2 KINGS 4:1-7

Our Father in Heaven, You have given us everything that we need. Thank You for this food and bless it to our bodies. Thank You that You have given us more than enough, with plenty to share. We thank You that our cupboards have never been bare. We bless You in the Name of the Lord. Amen!

Memory Verse: *"...for your Father knows what you need before you ask him."* (Matthew 6:8, ESV)

READ AND THINK ABOUT
PSALM 4

Dear God, I thank You that I can lie down to sleep in peace. Your watchful eye over me will never cease. When I awake, please take hold of me, to guard and to keep me. In all Your ways, guide me through all my days. Amen!

Memory Verse: *"We must obey God rather than men."*
(Acts 5:29, ESV)

READ AND THINK ABOUT

JOHN 11:28-44

Lord Jesus, You are very important to me.
I love You with my whole heart. Keep me close
to You. Protect me while I sleep. Amen!

Memory Verse: *"Prepare the way of the Lord;
make his paths straight."*
(Matthew 3:3, ESV)

2 SAMUEL 22:1-7

Dear God, thank You for keeping me this day.
Forgive me if I have done any wrong
or gone astray.
Please lead me into Your saving Truth
and keep me along Life's Way. Come
now to help me do what is right.
Keep me safe through the night. Amen!

Memory Verse: *"...be sure your sin
will find you out."*
(Numbers 32:23, ESV)

READ AND THINK ABOUT
2 SAMUEL 22:16-25

Dear God, as I lie down to sleep this night,
please keep my heart pure and white.
Send Your angels to my side, to
comfort me, all through the night.
Wake me with the cooing of the
mourning dove at daylight. Amen!

Memory Verse: *"Delight yourself in the Lord,
and he will give you the desires of your heart."*
(Psalm 37:4, ESV)

1 CHRONICLES 16:8-14

Dear Lord Jesus, Your face is what I seek.
Please give me a good night's sleep.
Please keep away bad dreams; I pray
for sweet dreams instead.
Thank You God for Your amazing love and
care, for You are with me everywhere.
Thank You God. Amen!

Memory Verse: *"Lead me to the
rock that is higher than I."*
(Psalm 61:2, ESV)

READ AND THINK ABOUT
2 SAMUEL 22:31-37

Dear God, thank You for being with me today. Thank You for loving me and for my family. Help me to be kind at work and at play. Help me to learn more of the good things with each new day. Stay close to me and correct my ways, and from evil protect me all of my days. Amen!

Memory Verse: *"And my God will supply every need of yours according to his riches in glory in Christ Jesus."*
(Philippians 4:19, ESV)

PSALM 36:5-9

Dear Lord Jesus, thank You for this beautiful, exciting and fun day. Thank You for the true friends I have made while at work and at play. Thank You for my family so loving and true. Thank You, God; we all put our trust in You. Keep watch over us all with sweet dreams through the night, and wake us with the singing birds at daylight. Amen!

Memory Verse: *"I will give thanks to the Lord with my whole heart."*
(Psalm 9:1, ESV)

PSALM 103:1-13

Dear God, it seems to be getting late.
It's after eight and night time won't wait.
Help me to remember to brush my teeth
when getting ready for bed. Lord, I need
You to refresh my tired weary head.
Thank You Lord for being with me today.
I think about all that's been said. I pray
that I did not say a careless word to
discourage or cause anyone to go astray.
O Lord, fill me with more of Your kindness
and more of Your love to give, that I may
please You every day that I live. Amen!

Memory Verse: *"Let the words of my
mouth and the meditation of my heart
be acceptable in your sight."*
(Psalm 19:14, ESV)

READ AND THINK ABOUT
MARK 5:35-43

Dear God, thank You for keeping us all safe another day. Thank You for my mommy and my daddy. They love me very much and care for me every day. Oh, how I love their gentle hugs and kisses on the cheek. I pray You will watch over us all while we sleep. Heavenly Father, Your love is so amazingly strong and yet tenderly sweet. All Your righteous ways we want to keep. Amen!

Memory Verse: *"...when I awake, I shall be satisfied with your likeness."* (Psalm 17:15, ESV)

MARK 10:46-52

Dear God, thank You for the wonderful day. We had much fun at play. You guided the words that we did say. Night time is near and I have tired sleepy eyes. Give us a good night's sleep. Wake us with the early morning sunrise. Thank you for the many mornings I've enjoyed with fresh peanut butter and honey on my toast. I like that the most. Let me hear Your tender whisper of love. I know that I am not alone. You are watching over us all from Your heavenly home. Amen!

Memory Verse: *"I am the light of the world. Whoever follows me will never walk in darkness, but will have the light of life."*
(John 8:12, NIV)

READ AND THINK ABOUT
PSALM 138

Dear Jesus, night time is almost here. Your moon and stars are shining brightly. I hear the bird's song coming from the bushes nearby. It's the song of the whippoorwill singing in the stillness of the coming night. I turn to You, Lord, and thank You for keeping me safe this day. You kept me from getting into a fight. You answered me when I called upon You with all my might. You quickly showed me a way for peace. From evil You did help me turn away. I thank You for Your still small voice that helped me make the right choice. Thank You God for this day and for keeping me from going astray. Oh how I love You, Lord Jesus. Amen!

Memory Verse: *"...how shall we escape if we neglect such a great salvation?"*
(Hebrews 2:3, ESV)

MORE PRAYERS

READ AND THINK ABOUT
MARK 1:9-22

Dear Lord Jesus, what joy You bring to my
heart in the morning! I am awakened by the
bluebirds singing and chirping as they call
out to You, Lord God. I too call out to You,
Lord. Hear my earnest prayer. Keep me
close to You. All Your ways are good. All Your
ways are sure. Thank You for taking care of
me. Your love never fails. Your love for me
never gives up. When I am in distress
and I don't know what to do,
You answer me when I call upon You—"Jesus."
Thank You that Your love never changes. It is
always the same, no matter where I am or
what I am doing. Jesus, I love You. Amen.

Memory Verse: *"Jesus Christ is the same
yesterday and today and forever."*
(Hebrews 13:8, ESV)

READ AND THINK ABOUT
MARK 4:35-41

Heavenly Father, thank You for the beautiful early morning sunrise. You control and have authority over the whole universe and the skies. You are an awesome God and I want to praise You. You are so big, so strong and so powerful. There is no one like You. Thank You for the way You have made me. You can help me in everything. You see and hear everything and everyone all at the same time. How wonderful You are. I put my trust in You because You know what is best for me all the time. Amen.

Memory Verse: *"I will never leave you nor forsake you."*
(Hebrews 13:5, ESV)

READ AND THINK ABOUT
PSALM 51:1-13

Dear God, You know my heart. Please make it clean. Give me a right spirit and a right attitude in all things. Fill my life with your goodness. I need Your saving power for me to live right. Help me to be productive in everything I do. Help me to do excellent things for Your good pleasure. May You rejoice over me with singing. Help me to honour You in the music I sing and listen to. Jesus, I praise You. You are my Lord and King. Amen.

Memory Verse: *"Create in me a clean heart, O God, and renew a right spirit within me."* (Psalm 51:10, ESV)

READ AND THINK ABOUT

PSALM 95

Dear Lord Jesus, I'm sorry for the wrong things I've done. Thank You for Your forgiveness. Change my heart so that I would change my selfish ways. Show me when I sin and remind me to confess it. Fill me with Your Holy Spirit so that I may practice good habits that would please You. I need Your help to begin to do things differently from what I have been used to. Jesus, I want my life to be honest and truthful. I am Your servant child. Give me Your understanding to know what to do and what Your will is for me. Amen.

Memory Verse: *"Oh come, let us worship and bow down; let us kneel before the Lord, our Maker!"*
(Psalm 95:6, ESV)

PSALM 84

Dear Lord God, please guide my heart and mind to have more of Your thoughts. *(Tell the Lord what you want to talk to Him about today.)* Give me wisdom to know the difference between what is right and what is wrong. Keep me from being deceived and doing wrong. But even much more than that, Lord, let Your Spirit guide me to know the difference between right and almost right. Help me to make the right choices. I put my trust in You, Jesus, and I am so happy to belong to You. Amen.

Memory Verse: *"Set your minds on things that are above, not on things that are on earth."* (Colossians 3:2, ESV)

READ AND THINK ABOUT
PSALM 86:1-12

Dear Lord Jesus, my Saviour, how good and forgiving You are to those who love and call upon Your Name. Holy Spirit, thank You for being my guardian and my guide. Please stay close to my side. May I find Your favour in all the choices that I make. It's all about You, Jesus, gently leading and clearing the way for me to take. Direct me into the right paths of life that would bring honour to You. Teach me Your ways and help me to know more about Your truth. Amen.

Memory Verse: *"If I had cherished sin in my heart, the Lord would not have listened..."* (Psalm 66:18, NIV)

NUMBERS 6:22-27

Dear Heavenly Father, thank You that You have brought much joy to my heart. May I never cause unhappiness to Your heart by displeasing You. If I should fail in any way by grieving Your Spirit, please forgive me. Help me Jesus. Draw me nearer to You, O Lord, I pray. I so much want to make the right choices that would bring honour to You. May my heart be refreshed as I feel Your presence. Let Your face shine down on me and help me in all I do. Draw me near to You so that I can make You happy, too. Amen.

Memory Verse: *"...looking to Jesus, the founder and perfecter of our faith..."*
(Hebrews 12:2, ESV)

READ AND THINK ABOUT
JOHN 10:22-30

*What do you want to talk to the
Lord about today?*

O Lord, You hold me in the palm of Your hand.
With each new day there is safety as I
lovingly obey Your command.
You are so big, mighty and strong.
With You I rejoice to belong. Amen.

Memory Verse: *"Love never fails."*
(1 Corinthians 13:8, NIV)

PHILIPPIANS 2:1-11

Dear Lord Jesus, You are a wonderful
Saviour to me. Your Name is power
and is above every name.
What a beautiful and wonderful name.
By Your Name, You have saved me. You keep
me from all sin and shame. I praise Your Holy
Name. Fill me with the mind of Christ.
Help me to humbly serve others, not
pushing for my own way. I just want to
talk to You, Lord, and say: Take me, make
me and mold me as You are the potter and
I am the clay. Jesus, have Your own
perfect way in me. Amen.

Memory Verse: *Jesus said to him: "I am the way,
and the truth, and the life. No one comes
to the Father except through me."*
(John 14:6, ESV)

READ AND THINK ABOUT
ISAIAH 6:1-7

Dear Lord Jesus, how majestic is Your Name in all of heaven and earth. You are high and lifted up. You are full of truth and You do not lie. Forgive me for telling lies—even those small white lies. Come and touch my mouth and my lips. I do not want to practice telling any type of lies even though others around me tell lies. Please help me to live holy and truthful. I want to be reliable and useful. Fill me with Your truth and never let me go. I want to become more like You, Jesus, full of truth. Amen.

Memory Verse: *"Holy, holy, holy is the Lord of hosts; the whole earth is full of his glory!"* (Isaiah 6:3, ESV)

READ AND THINK ABOUT
1 CORINTHIANS 1:4-9

Dear God, thank You that You hear and answer prayer. Help me to keep my heart in prayer. You lovingly care and are with me everywhere. When I am tempted to do wrong or bad things, please help me to say 'no'. Holy Spirit speak to me so that I hear what You have to say. Rescue me and guide me along a better way. Thank You, Lord, for Your plan is most secure. Keep my faith strong and pure. Build me up in You, Jesus. You will never let me down for sure. You are still faithful like You always were. Amen.

Memory Verse: *"Watch and pray that you may not enter into temptation. The spirit indeed is willing, but the flesh is weak."* (Matthew 26:41, ESV)

JOHN 10:1-9

Dear Holy Spirit, You speak to me often. I cherish the times when You whisper Your love to me. Help me to wait in prayer more and listen to You as You speak Your word into my heart. When I ask You Lord: *"What should I pray?"* You always tell me. Help me to study Your word so that I recognize when You are speaking to me. Help me to listen to Your ways so that I do not make bad mistakes. You love me so much and I love You too. Jesus, I want to grow up being a follower of You. Amen.

Memory Verse: *"My sheep hear my voice, and I know them, and they follow me."* (John 10:27, ESV)

READ AND THINK ABOUT
ROMANS 8:26-39

Dear Holy Spirit, what a joy to have You as
my counsellor, my comforter and my guide.
You talk with me. You show me things that are
hidden from me that I do not know. You show
me what to do. May I learn to seek the face
of Jesus Christ. Lord, Your love for me never
changes. Nothing can separate us
from Your love. How I long for my heart
to grow stronger in You. Rescue me from
any troubles or temptation that would
cause trouble in my life. Keep me true,
Lord Jesus. Keep me true to You. Amen.

Memory Verse: *"....nor anything else in all
creation, will be able to separate us from the
love of God that is in Christ Jesus our Lord."*
(Romans 8:39, NIV)

MARK 4:1-9

Dear Lord Jesus, I have been having such a struggle to pray. My heart is not right when sometimes I forget about You. I have been doing things on the sly secretly to make things work out the way I want them to. I have been dishonest and disobedient to You. Lord, I cannot hide this sin from You. You see everything and know everything I am doing. Please forgive me and help me to be honest even in the small things. Help me to think and live honestly to please You.
Keep me close to You. Amen.

Memory Verse: *"If we confess our sins, he is faithful and just to forgive us our sins and to cleanse us from all unrighteousness."*
(1 John 1:9, ESV)

LUKE 18:35-43

Dear God, I thank You for taking care of me in so many ways. You know how rude I have been to others. I am sorry. Please forgive me. Help me to share kindness in my thoughts and in my words. May my actions prove to be loyal and true. When I face hard and difficult times help me to remember to call out to You, Jesus. You are always with me to help me. You know what is best for me in the end. Please help me to always seek the presence of Your Holy Spirit. I put my faith and trust in You. Amen.

Memory Verse: *"Trust in the Lord with all your heart and lean not on your own understanding..."*
(Proverbs 3:5, NIV)

READ AND THINK ABOUT
ROMANS 5:1-9

Dear God, You are so loving and wonderful to me. I bring You my brokenness and sinful shame. Forgive me and take away the embarrassing pain. You have covered me with Your precious blood at Calvary, so please help my faith to be strong. May I experience true freedom in Christ; freedom from the guilt of sin and wrong. Wash my heart and the eyes of my heart. Holy Spirit pour over me the blessed way of correction. Draw me nearer to You and surround me with Your loving kindness and tender affection. Amen.

Memory Verse: *"...but God shows his love for us in that while we were still sinners, Christ died for us."*
(Romans 5:8, ESV)

READ AND THINK ABOUT
PSALM 27:1-6

Dear Jesus, I thank You for my parents. Help me to honour and respect them. I want to obey them with a right and joyful attitude. Help them to always have work that pays to support the family. Keep us all near to Your heart, O God, so that we have no fear. Let nothing separate us. I thank You for the times when we come together to love and support one another. Thank You for the times when we can laugh and enjoy each another's company, and even shed a few tears if we have to part for a while. Jesus, there is no one like You, keeping us together as one happy family. Thank You for Your keeping power. O how I love You. Amen.

Memory Verse: *"One thing have I asked of the Lord, that will I seek after: that I may dwell in the house of the Lord all the days of my life."* (Psalm 27:4, ESV)

READ AND THINK ABOUT
ROMANS 12:9-21

Dear God, thank You for my brother/s and/or sister/s. *(Name your brother/s and/or sister/s.)* Help me to respect them, being tender and kind to them even when it is hard to do. Please help us not to argue or get into a fight, for that would displease You and bring shame on us. Let Your compassionate love in us be strong for each other. May we be quick to forgive when we need to. Let generosity increase among us. O God, with Your help, we as a family can live together in harmony. Thank You for helping us. Amen.

Memory Verse: *"Do everything without complaining or arguing, so that you may become blameless and pure, children of God..."*
(Philippians 2:14-15, NIV)

PSALM 139:1-10

Dear God, I thank You for all of my family. I appreciate them. They teach me how to live for Jesus Christ. I praise You for Your wonderful works. Help me to take responsibility in keeping my room clean and tidy and in hanging up my clothes. You know everything about me. I pray that I will not be idle or thoughtless, nor waste time. Fill me with joy as I do my work. Lord, You know the ways that I take and when You have tested me, with Your help, I shall come forth as gold. Lord, build my character so I will stay strong and bold. Amen.

Memory Verse: *"For my thoughts are not your thoughts, neither are your ways my ways, declares the Lord."*
(Isaiah 55:8, ESV)

ISAIAH: 58:6-11

Dear God, I now come to You with a joyful
and thankful heart. I thank You for my
grandparents. *(Name them.)* Thank You for
their true kindness to us. Lord, please make
them more healthy and strong. Keep their
hearts and minds clear. Let true love and
faithfulness be their strength through all their
years. Clothe us all in Your garments white for
the remainder of our years. May we continue
to serve You. O how I love You, Jesus.
Keep us all close to You. Amen.

Memory Verse: *"Owe nothing to anyone
except to love one another..."*
(Romans 13:8, NASB)

READ AND THINK ABOUT
TITUS 3:1-11

Dear Lord Jesus, thank You for making Your salvation available to all our family. Help us to continue to look out for one another, to guide and protect one another. May we encourage one another and build each other up. Help us to show mercy and not to condemn or criticize anyone. Let our faith in Christ be increased, and our love toward each other grow even more. O Father in Heaven, let there be no unforgiving attitude in any of us, so that nothing can block our prayers from being answered. Keep us full of the truth in our hearts, and may we always be quick to forgive. In Jesus' Name I pray. Amen.

Memory Verse: *"Above all else, guard your heart, for it is the wellspring of life."*
(Proverbs 4:23, NIV)

PSALM 98:1-6

Dear Heavenly Father, thank You for protecting us in all our travelling—at home on the busy highways, in different parts of the country, or even to a new country. Thank You for sending Your angels to guard us and take charge over us. Give us opportunity to explore and adventure to new places. When the language is unfamiliar to us, give us people who are able to communicate and help us. You know when it is the best time for us to travel. Lead us to the places You want us to go. Lord, show us how to get there. Amen.

Memory Verse: *"Ask, and it will be given to you; seek, and you will find; knock, and it will be opened to you."*
(Matthew 7:7, ESV)

READ AND THINK ABOUT
PHILIPPIANS 4:4-13

Dear God, sin has caused my parents to go apart. My heart is heavy and torn and in shock. I know my parents argued a lot. Please forgive their sin and cause them to forgive each other. Please bring about a change and a new love for each other. Lord Jesus, please show me how to live and the right things to do. I just want to cry and cry to You. Help me to be strong. Let me hide myself in You. Oh Lord, come and heal my aching heart. We all need You and are trusting in You for a fresh start. Amen.

Memory Verse: *"Jesus wept."*
(John 11:35, ESV)

READ AND THINK ABOUT
1 JOHN 3:16-24

Dear Heavenly Father, You are a God of amazing love. Help me to adjust to my parent's separation. Show me how to live when going back and forth from my mother's home to my father's home. Lord, this is very hard for me. Don't let sadness rule my life. Help me not to take sides, but to love and honour both parents. I just can't understand why they can't love each other. I love them both. Fill me more with Your Holy Spirit. Teach me how to live above this trouble. I love You Lord, for I can depend on You. Amen.

Memory Verse: *"...let your light shine before others, so that they may see your good works and give glory to your Father who is in heaven."* (Matthew 5:16, ESV)

READ AND THINK ABOUT
JOHN 14:15-27

Dear Lord Jesus, I am so glad that You are my closest friend. You understand all that happens to me. Everyone around me seems so unfriendly. I seem to have no friends. But, somehow Jesus, help me to kindly reach out and make friends. You can show me how. Forgive me for all my pride, for thinking I am always right. Hold me in Your loving arms very tight. Wash over me till my heart is white. Show me how to do what is right. Fill my heart with Your sunshine bright. Jesus, I need You to help me live in Your light. Amen.

Memory Verse: *"This is My commandment,
that you love one another,
just as I have loved you."*
(John 15:12, NASB)

READ AND THINK ABOUT

ROMANS 10:13-17

Dear Lord Jesus, today I want to pray for my friends. Holy Spirit, draw their hearts close to You. Help me to share God's wonderful love with them. Open their eyes to see the love of Jesus, whose name they have never yet heard. Open their hearts and mind to believe in You and receive You. Forgive their sins and remove from them any misunderstanding or unbelief so that they will no longer be deceived or fooled by Satan, the devil. Help them to accept You, Jesus, to see that You died and gave Your very life for them. Jesus, I ask You to please save my friends. Amen.

Memory Verse: *"...everyone who calls on the name of the Lord will be saved."* (Romans 10:13, ESV)

ROMANS 10:1-13

Dear God, I think of all the wonderful things You have done for me. You fill my heart with great joy. I pray for my friends that they, too, would receive the joy of Your salvation. May they come to know and to love You. Lord, forgive them of their sins and many faults. Take away the false ways that would mislead them down wrong paths to destruction. Holy Spirit, speak into their hearts. May they hear You calling them to be a Christian. I pray they choose to follow You and obey Your commands. Thank You, Lord, for answering my prayer. Amen.

Memory Verse: *"...if you confess with your mouth that Jesus is Lord and believe in your heart that God raised him from the dead, you will be saved."*
(Romans 10:9, ESV)

ISAIAH 55:1-7

Dear God, I continue to pray for my dear friends, whom I love. Holy Spirit, draw their hearts close to Your heart. May they seek You and call upon You while You are near. I ask You, O Father in Heaven, soften their hearts towards You. May their hearts long for You and become thirsty for the living word of God. Forgive their sins. Take away all fear as they call upon Your holy name. Cause my friends to make a decision to follow You before it is too late. Jesus, I pray they would be ready when You come. Amen.

Memory Verse: *"Seek the Lord while he may be found; call upon him while he is near."*
(Isaiah 55:6, ESV)

ROMANS 1:9-17

Dear Lord Jesus, I am desperate for You. You are my friend. Jesus, I want to tell You about my friends because they are lost without You. My heart cries out. O God, may they pay attention to You. You are the mighty One and great in power. Give them the faith to believe and trust in You even this very hour. Forgive them of their sin. God, You have the power for their salvation. May they choose to follow You, Jesus Christ. Help them to see how You love them still. Holy Spirit, come in power for us all this very hour. Amen.

Memory Verse: *"For I am not ashamed of the gospel, for it is the power of God for salvation to everyone who believes..."* (Romans 1:16, ESV)

2 CORINTHIANS 6:14-18, 7:1

Dear Jesus, You alone are my king. You are exalted high above everything. In the heavens, You rule on Your glorious throne. Give to me true friends that will love You and follow You. Lord Jesus, make known to them Your righteous ways. May we all be true with one another. May we all be sincere in obeying Your commands and encouraging each other. Forgive me of any secret sins and also any unknown sin. Fill me with Your Holy Spirit; may I begin to find a new and deeper walk with You. Amen.

Memory Verse: *"...if anyone is in Christ, he is a new creation. The old has passed away; behold, the new has come."*
(2 Corinthians 5:17, ESV)

READ AND THINK ABOUT
ISAIAH 55:6-13

Dear Lord Jesus, I just want to thank You for the wonderful friends You have given to me. I pray that my friends remain true and faithful to You, dear Lord. I thank You that we have so much in common and are so much like-minded. We like to do things together and we like each other's company. Jesus, I am happy that they love You too. May our friendships last forever. Jesus, You also are my forever friend. Amen.

Memory Verse: *"Let this mind be in you which was also in Christ Jesus."*
(Philippians 2:5, NKJV)

MATTHEW 26:69-75

Dear Jesus, You are the God who saves and keeps me. You never change and You will forever be. I know that You are the one who always loves and cares for me. While my friends may prove to be untrue, I am happy that I belong to You. You never disappoint me and You never fail me. Though my friends may sometimes be few, help me to draw nearer to You. You bring comfort and peace to me like no one else could ever do. That's why I desire to trust You more. Amen.

Memory Verse: *"...but there is a friend who sticks closer than a brother."*
(Proverbs 18:24, ESV)

READ AND THINK ABOUT
LUKE 12:22-31

Dear God, You are awesome and wonderful. You always supply our needs in an amazing way. Even before we ask, the answer is on the way. You give us plenty of food to eat and even extra for a treat. Thank You for warm clothes to wear. You have even given us an extra pair. You've kept our bodies healthy and strong. We ask You to keep us from all evil and wrong. You are our God in whom we treasure, and in You we find great pleasure. Amen.

Memory Verse: *"I have come that they may have life, and that they may have it more abundantly."* (John 10:10, NKJV)

DANIEL 1:9-21

Dear Lord God, You have amazing wisdom. You are a God of peace. You understand my ways, which are sometimes not so thoughtful or smart. I pray, God, that You would help me to care for my body. Help me not to desire junk food, but give me an appetite for more vegetables and even broccoli. Lord Jesus, I need more faith in You to build me up to develop good eating habits. Help me to also exercise regularly. Your grace can empower me and enable me to do that which I find hard. I thank You, Lord, that I can depend on You. Amen.

Memory Verse: *"Not by might, nor by power, but by my Spirit, says the Lord of hosts."* (Zechariah 4:6, ESV)

READ AND THINK ABOUT
PSALM 145:8-21

Dear Lord God, thank You for Your healing power. You know just what we need at the right time. You satisfy our desires in all kinds of surprising ways. We hope for excellent, quick healing, and for Your safety for all our days. You desire for our hearts to be full of compassion for others, just like You have compassion for us. I want to follow Your righteous plans. Help us to follow hand in hand with You, Jesus, and tightly hold onto Your nail-scarred hands. Amen.

Memory Verse: *"Do not be anxious about anything, but in everything, by prayer and petition, with thanksgiving, present your requests to God."*
(Philippians 4:6, NIV)

PSALM 46

Dear Lord God, thank You for being the great healer. Thank You for hearing us when we pray. We need Your joy to keep us through this trial and pain. Keep us strong so that we do not fall apart. I surrender to You all of my aching heart. I surrender my mind, emotions and my own will. What's on my mind I give to You in exchange for Your thoughts. I give You my emotions for Your peace. I give You my will for Your loving kindness. Come bless my soul. Make my life fully whole. Amen.

Memory Verse: *"Be still, and know that I am God."*
(Psalm 46:10, ESV)

PSALM 37:1-9

Dear God, I thank You that You care so much for me. I come to tell You about many things. My heart is crushed and broken. All I can do is cry to You. I cannot find the words to be spoken. God, I know You can heal all my sorrow and pain. So take my heart, Lord, my heavy heart, in Jesus' name. Your life You gave for me at Calvary, and my burdens You took there to bear. Please carry me with Your tender love and care. Lord, You have endless joy for me as I wait with You in prayer. Amen.

Memory Verse: *"A joyful heart is good medicine, but a crushed spirit dries up the bones."*
(Proverbs 17:22, ESV)

READ AND THINK ABOUT
HOSEA 6:1-3

Dear Father in Heaven, thank You for hearing my prayer. I give thanks to You because You already know all about the sad things that concern me. I pray for: *(Name the things to pray about.)* I ask You, Lord, for healing. You are able to make a difference in all our days. You carry the weight of our sorrow. You give us so much hope for a better tomorrow. Holy Spirit, pour Your healing over us. Like a refreshing rain, come to comfort and heal all our pain. Lord, I ask for healing in Jesus' name. Amen.

Memory Verse: *"You are my hiding place and my shield; I hope in your word."*
(Psalm 119:114, ESV)

READ AND THINK ABOUT
MATTHEW 5:1-12

Holy Spirit, You are our greatest comforter and
healer. Our family is torn and we need Your
comfort. Lord Jesus, bind us together in
Your tender loving arms so sweetly. For
cries of sadness flood our eyes with tears
as we fondly remember the past years.
Fill our hearts and minds with precious
memories to comfort and keep as we weep.
For You will not leave us in despair. Come and
surround us and carry us through each day
with Your gentle loving care. Amen.

Memory Verse: *"Blessed are those who mourn,
for they shall be comforted."*
(Matthew 5:4, NASB)

EPHESIANS 6:10-18

Dear Lord Jesus, You are my Lord and King. You are in control of everything. You give me the strength to face the trials that You permit to come my way. Lord, I ask You to spare me and heal me from the sickness and the pain that attacks my body. *(Name the sickness and/or pain.)* Forgive me of all my sin. I also forgive those who have sinned against me. Restore my body and soul and make me whole. You are the greatest healer. There is none like You. In You, Jesus, every day is better than the one before. Oh, how I want to love You more and more. Amen.

Memory Verse: *"For God so loved the world that he gave his one and only Son, that whoever believes in him shall not perish but have eternal life."*
(John 3:16, NIV)

READ AND THINK ABOUT
1 PETER 1:13-25

Dear God, You are highest, the greatest and the strongest. You are holy, and You desire for me to be holy too. Lord Jesus, You bought me and redeemed me with Your precious blood when You bled and died on the cross for me. Deliver me and keep me from evil all my days. God, You are perfect in all Your ways. Set me apart to live for godly purposes all my life. Holy Spirit, protect me and keep me walking close to Your side. May I always abide in Your word. I want to live my life for You all my days. Amen.

Memory Verse: *"In all your ways acknowledge Him, and He will make your paths straight."*
(Proverbs 3:6, NASB)

PSALM 1

Dear God, thank You for Your holy Name. It is like a strong tower. In Your Name there is awesome power. Hallelujah! Hallelujah! You are still the same. You came to bring new life to me, to take away the bad and bring about the good. Help me to live and pray each day as I should. I seek You, as I want to be holy and more like you. Set me apart from the way of sinners, that I may dwell in Your presence and be amongst the winners. I bless Your holy and wonderful Name. Amen.

Memory Verse: *"...it is written, 'Be holy, for I am holy.'"*
(1 Peter 1:16, NKJV)

READ AND THINK ABOUT
1 JOHN 3:1-10

Dear God, You are holy. Make me pure and holy too. Lord, I can't even imagine how holy You are. Jesus, I want to be more holy, like You. You make me happy, and I want to make people happy too. Separate me from the things of the world that would bring unhappiness and cause me to be discontent. Whenever that happens, please show me the error of my ways that I may repent. Keep me away from hurtful things. Hide me safely under your wings. Amen.

Memory Verse: *"But the fruit of the Spirit is love, joy, peace, patience, kindness, goodness, faithfulness, gentleness, self-control..."*
(Galatians 5:22-23, ESV)

READ AND THINK ABOUT

COLOSSIANS 3:1-10

Dear Lord Jesus, You are the one who makes me holy. Come and separate me from worldly ways. You have wonderful thoughts for me. Set my mind and thoughts on heavenly things above—give me thoughts that are true and right, lovely and pure. Direct me in the ways that are most safe and secure. Keep me from evil quarrelling and unkind speech. Lord Jesus, I want to practice only what You teach. Your knowledge is real, with precious promises that are true. That is why I want to follow You my whole life through. Amen.

Memory Verse: *"For by grace you have been saved through faith. And this is not your own doing; it is the gift of God."*
(Ephesians 2:8, ESV)

READ AND THINK ABOUT
ISAIAH 26:3-9

Dear Lord God, I thank You for being in control of everything. You know what tomorrow brings. Help me not to associate with friends who would not be good for me and who may not be reliable. Keep me close to You, doing things that are most desirable. Help me to remember to read my Bible so that I can understand it. It is full of truth and I believe in what it says. Holy Spirit, speak to me as I read it. Let me know You are near. Amen.

Memory Verse: *"Trust in the Lord forever, for the Lord God is an everlasting rock."*
(Isaiah 26:4, ESV)

PSALM 119:1-16

Dear Father in Heaven, You have given me the Bible, Your holy word. Holy Spirit, teach me and show me, from Your Word, heavenly things that I have never before heard. Help me to know how You want me to live according to Your righteous standards. I put my faith in You, Christ Jesus, and I thank You for putting Your righteousness upon me. Help me not to turn away from Your commands, but to cherish them in my heart. May I understand what You want me to see. I praise and thank You for Your Holy Word. It helps to keep me from all wrong, and makes me bold and strong. Amen.

Memory Verse: *"I have stored up your word in my heart, that I might not sin against you."*
(Psalm 119:11, ESV)

2 TIMOTHY 3:12-17

Dear God, thank You for the Bible. It is the best book. It teaches me how to prepare to meet You. Thank You for giving me a mind that can learn and memorize. Help me not to day dream or be idle, but to take the time to read and study the Bible. The Bible does not lie to us; it is full of truth for healthy living. It is alive and will never pass away. Thank You, Jesus, that I have discovered You and received the Holy Spirit to live in me. Holy Spirit, may I hear You speaking into my heart as I read Your word. Amen.

Memory Verse: *"Man shall not live by bread alone, but by every word that comes from the mouth of God."*
(Matthew 4:4, ESV)

READ AND THINK ABOUT
ISAIAH 43:18-19

Dear God, You fill my way every day with love. It is so precious to know that I am loved by You. Lord, You keep me smiling and You bring peace and quietness to my life. Separate me from the worldly noise, like too much T.V and all the unnecessary toys. Lord, sometimes too much stuff keeps me from praying and reading Your word enough. Lord, give me quietness to search my heart. Allow the selfish wants in me to slowly depart. I want more of Your love, Jesus, living in my heart. Amen.

Memory Verse: *"Your word is a lamp to my feet and a light to my path."* (Psalm 119:105, ESV)

READ AND THINK ABOUT
1 SAMUEL 16:1-13

Dear Lord God, thank You for my school classmates. Help me to be kind to each one of them. In class time, help me to be diligent in doing my schoolwork. May I always pay attention to what's being taught. During spare time, help me to keep focused on my work so that I do not daydream. Help me to know when to talk and when to be quiet. Jesus, fill me with Your genuine loving kindness and gentleness. May I shine for You, Jesus. Amen.

Memory Verse: *"...love covers a multitude of sins."*
(1 Peter 4:8, NASB)

HEBREWS 12:7-13

Dear God, thank You for being with me always. Lord, I struggle and have difficulty concentrating on my schoolwork. Help me not to be distracted from doing it. Please come alongside me when I am in class. Help me not to waste time or daydream. Help me to work diligently. I know You can help me to change my ways, and it's not too late. Lord Jesus, on You I can depend. You are able to help me to receive good marks in the end. Thank You God for the helpful answer You will send. Amen.

Memory Verse: *"For we are God's workmanship, created in Christ Jesus to do good works, which God prepared in advance for us to do."* (Ephesians 2:10, NIV)

READ AND THINK ABOUT
PSALM 90:12-17

Dear God, thank You for Your awesome power.
You guide and help me every day and every
hour. With Your power I can pass all school
tests and exams. Lord Jesus, help me improve
my reading. Take away the desire to spend so
much time with computer games. Keep me
from watching violent things that only bring
about shame and loss. Thank You for giving
Your life for me on the cross. I surrender my will
to You and let You be my boss. Holy Spirit, lead
me so I shall never suffer any loss. Amen.

Memory Verse: *"Humble yourselves before
the Lord, and he will exalt you."*
(James 4:10, ESV)

LUKE 24:13-23

Dear God in Heaven, thank You I can go to school riding the school bus. Help me not to be late but on time to catch the bus. I thank You for all the bus drivers. Help them to be careful. Protect us all on the bus. Help us all to respect and pay attention to what the bus driver says. May we all stay in our seats and not cause trouble on the bus. Lord, I know you come along and ride the bus with us. You are with us everywhere—even on the bus. Thank You Lord. Amen.

Memory Verse: *"...be strong in the Lord and in the strength of his might."* (Ephesians 6:10, ESV)

READ AND THINK ABOUT
PSALM 32:1-8

Dear Lord Jesus, You are the greatest teacher in the whole wide world. You teach the way of truth that heals and builds me up. My heart rejoices in You so much that I want to give loud praises to You with a loud shout. Teach me, O Lord, in the way that I should go. When You have shown the way for me to go, please help me to surrender all my will to Yours. May I walk and live in Your truth. With my heart united in Your name, I will never be the same. Amen.

Memory Verse: *"I will instruct you and teach you in the way you should go; I will counsel you and watch over you."*
(Psalm 32:8, NIV)

MATTHEW 12:33-37

Dear God, You are sovereign and You rule over everything. I pray for the teachers in my school. May they have Your favour resting upon them. Allow them to teach what is true and fair. Help me to be respectful to them. Help me to discern what is true and what is false. O God, I am what I am and how You made me. I am made in the image of God. Let no one try to change that. God, You are perfect in all of Your ways. You created me wonderfully. Lord Jesus, may the teachers honour all Your creation and follow Your commands. Amen.

Memory Verse: *"...without faith it is impossible to please God..."*
(Hebrews 11:6, NIV)

READ AND THINK ABOUT
PSALM 46:1-7

Dear God, I thank You for being with me all the time. You are my friend. Today, I really need You. I have been very disappointed lately. *(Name the disappointment.)* I feel so very blue. My heart is crushed and sorrowful. You are my faithful friend and I can depend on You. Please come and take away my grief and heal my aching heart. Jesus, fill my life with your amazing love from heaven above. Make my life complete once again and fill me with Your joy. Help me to be what You want me to be. Amen.

Memory Verse: *"God is our refuge and strength, a very present help in trouble."*
(Psalm 46:1, ESV)

ROMANS 5:1-5

Dear Lord Jesus, Your care for me is so wonderful and I thank You. It has been a difficult time for me. I missed the opportunity of reaching my goal. I just feel sick to my soul. I am feeling sad and let down, as I have fallen short of my expectations. I feel so disappointed. Lord Jesus, help me to trust in You even when I don't understand why these things happen. You took my sad and hurt feelings when You were on the cross. You cared so much for me. Now my soul waits for Your strength to bring joy and happiness back to me. Amen.

Memory Verse: *"And we know that God causes all things to work together for good to those who love God, to those who are called according to His purpose."* (Romans 8:28, NASB)

JOHN 15:1-11

Dear Lord God, You know what is in my heart today. Please show me why I am feeling so discontented. Sins like these: *(resentment, envy, pride, boastfulness, anger, lying, or any other sins)* are not meant to be in my heart. Help me not to be greedy or to steal—*even in small things.* Refresh my spirit and make my thoughts and heart pure. You love and value me. Help me to clean up my life. When I read the Bible, help me to understand it. You brought Your salvation for me to find it. Hold me in Your arms as I fix my eyes upon the cross. My life in You, Jesus, will never be lost. Amen.

Memory Verse: *"For the wages of sin is death, but the free gift of God is eternal life in Christ Jesus our Lord."*
(Romans 6:23, ESV)

ROMANS 6:15-23

Dear Lord Jesus, something has gone terribly wrong. I just can't explain it now but maybe farther along. Please forgive me. Guard my steps and set me free, so that sin no longer has a hold on me. I lean on You, Lord Jesus, that I may be strong and stand secure. Thank You, Lord Jesus. You alone are my anchor I can hold onto. Please come and help me as I lean on You. In Your everlasting arms I find my way, safe and secure with You. Amen.

Memory Verse: *"If you abide in me, and my words abide in you, ask whatever you wish, and it will be done for you."* (John 15:7, ESV)

READ AND THINK ABOUT
PSALM 123

Dear Holy Spirit, You are my strength and my comforter. I need Your comfort right now. Everyone is picking on me. I'm feeling very lonely and I am as sad as can be. I'm beginning to feel like I just don't belong. Jesus, I call on You to correct this situation before long. Nothing is too difficult for You. Fill me with Your Holy Spirit's power. Give me strong kindness that I may be polite and win back friendships that have gone sour. Forgive them for being so rude and making things unpleasant. Lord, You can bring the answer for I know You are always present. Amen.

Memory Verse: *"...fear not, for I am with you; be not dismayed, for I am your God; I will strengthen you, I will help you..."*
(Isaiah 41:10, ESV)

PSALM 86:1-12

Dear God, You are so great and full of kindness. From my enemies You shield and protect me. I ask You to please deliver me from the bullies who call me unkind names. They try to make me afraid. Help me and comfort me when they act hatefully and say hurtful words. Come and change their hearts, O God. May they be ashamed and turn away from their sin. Turn to me, O Lord, and be merciful and gracious to me. You are my anchor. Let me hide myself in You. Amen.

Memory Verse: *"In the day of my trouble I call upon you, for you answer me."* (Psalm 86:7, ESV)

READ AND THINK ABOUT
PSALM 116:1-9

Dear Jesus, oh how I love You. I cry out to You. I know You can hear my cry. Place Your tender arms around me. You already know the reasons why I cry. *(Tell the Lord your request.)* I call on Your Name, Jesus. In Your Name, Jesus, the enemy has to flee from me. Your Name is mighty and strong. In Your Name, I too become strong. Others will see that in Your Name I am kept from all wrong. Thank You, Jesus, that You heard my prayer. I feel much better now and I am in Your peace and everlasting care. Amen.

Memory Verse: *"The name of the Lord is a strong tower; the righteous man runs into it and is safe."*
(Proverbs 18:10, ESV)

READ AND THINK ABOUT
LUKE 15:1-10

Dear God, I cry out to You because I need You.
I have lost something very valuable to me.
(Name what is lost.) God, You know where it
is, and I would like it back. This is causing me
so much frustration. I cry out to You to come
and change my heart and situation. In the
meantime, I know You will take care of it. Lord,
You are my friend and I can talk to You about
it. I turn my eyes to You. I want to know more
about You. Your love is true and I am so
glad I can depend on You. Amen.

Memory verse: *"But seek first the kingdom
of God and his righteousness, and all
these things will be added to you."*
(Matthew 6:33, ESV)

READ AND THINK ABOUT
MATTHEW 6:25-34

Dear God, I praise You because everything comes from You. You know all about what tomorrow brings. All my worries and fears I give to You. They are too much for me to bear. *(Name the things that you are worried about.)* Lord, You are with me. Help me not to be anxious about these things. Remind me, Lord, to trust in You about everything. Every good gift comes from You at the right time. You give us everything we need. You are the God of plenty and have more than enough. Thank You, O Lord, because my future belongs to You and You have everything in control. Fill me with hope, joy and peace. Come and refresh my heart and my soul. Amen.

Memory Verse: *"...casting all your care upon Him, for He cares for you."*
(1 Peter 5:7, NKJV)

JOHN 14:1-6

Dear Lord Jesus, thank You for living inside of me. I do not have to be afraid to die because You are in me and I am in You. I let go of my own ways. I give up my selfish ambition. My life is not my own, but belongs to You. Because You have risen from the dead, I know I too will rise to a new life in heaven after I leave this earth. Whether I live or whether I die, I know You will still be with me forever. Jesus, I love You so very much. Amen.

Memory Verse: *"Whoever has the Son has life; whoever does not have the Son of God does not have life."*
(1 John 5:12, ESV)

READ AND THINK ABOUT
ISAIAH 41:8-13

Dear Lord God, thank You for being so good to me and always with me. Lord God, I still have some fears and I am sometimes afraid. *(Name what you are afraid of.)* Please take care of me, no matter the situation that arises. For in You, O God, there are no surprises. You know about everything ahead of time. Please guard me and go ahead of me so I won't fear. I choose to follow You because in You I am safe. Jesus, I surrender my all to You. O Lord, please make me to be more like You. Amen.

Memory Verse: *"For God has not given us a spirit of fear, but of power and of love and of a sound mind."*
(2 Timothy 1:7, NKJV)

PSALM 143

Dear God, You have awesome keeping power. You control all that happens in all the earth, in the heavens and the skies. You send the rain and the storms with thunder and lightning too. Sometimes the loud thunder frightens me and I am so afraid. Please keep me safe until the storm passes by. You are a great, great God. You guide and satisfy me. Thank You for keeping me safe in Jesus' name. Amen.

Memory Verse: *"You keep him in perfect peace whose mind is stayed on you, because he trusts in you."*
(Isaiah 26:3, ESV)

READ AND THINK ABOUT
1 CHRONICLES 14:8-17

Dear Heavenly Father, You are the God of the impossible. You can make good things happen even in difficult times. When I face challenges or threats, please help me to inquire from You first. Help me to wait on You in prayer until I receive specific direction on what to do. Make me strong, fearless and calm. Help me know more and more of Your living word. Nothing compares to Your voice to be heard. For all my days, may I inquire from You first and pray with Your word. Amen.

Memory Verse: *"For all who are led by the Spirit of God are sons of God."*
(Romans 8:14, ESV)

1 SAMUEL 3:1-10

Dear Lord Jesus, I can't help but think about all the good things You have been giving to us. You are amazing, God. I am well-blessed today. Sometimes, I think about the future. Lord, even though I am still young, I often wonder what I should be when I grow up. So I ask You, Lord: *"What do You want me to do when I grow up?"* I want to be in Your perfect will. Please prepare me in the best way possible. I pray for Your wonderful joy to bubble up inside me as You lead me day by day. Amen.

Memory Verse: *"This is the confidence we have in approaching God: that if we ask anything according to his will, he hears us."*
(1 John 5:14, NIV)

MATTHEW 7:24-29

Dear God, You are the Rock of my salvation. I want to build my life on You, Jesus. When I grow up, should I decide to marry, please prepare the right person for me. Let that person be full of the Holy Spirit. Let that person have much joy and love for You, O God, and also for me. May we be faithful and true to each other. Keep me in a good circle of friends. Help me to draw near to You always. Help me to make all the right choices with Your approval. Prepare me for my future days, in Jesus' name. Amen.

Memory Verse: *"Keep me as the apple of your eye; hide me in the shadow of your wings."* (Psalm 17:8, ESV)

MATTHEW 11:25-30

Dear Father God, You are holy with wisdom and understanding. You know all about my body and soul. I have obstacles and difficult decisions to make at this time. You know all things from beginning to end. I hear Your voice calling softly and tenderly. Lord, please lead me, as the future is unknown to me. You know the best way for me. Keep the way clear, let nothing interfere. Come and take my heart and go with me as I willingly follow Your Spirit. Thank You, God, You are never too late but always on time. Amen.

Memory Verse: *"For my yoke is easy, and my burden is light."*
(Matthew 11:30, ESV)

READ AND THINK ABOUT
ECCLESIASTES 5:1-7

Dear God, I thank You and pray for the church and for the Sunday school. May the leaders speak and teach the truth about God's love to us. Holy Spirit, help me to understand the teaching of the word. Increase my faith in You as I hear more about the miracles and healings of Jesus. May the church encourage me and show me how to live right. May there be support and care for one another. Lord, You care so much for all of us. Oh how I love You, Jesus. Amen.

Memory Verse: *"...though your sins are like scarlet, they shall be as white as snow..."* (Isaiah 1:18, ESV)

READ AND THINK ABOUT
MATTHEW 6:1-15

Dear Heavenly Father, thank You for the ways
You guide me. Give me the strength to do the
special tasks that You are calling me to do. I
want to help the poor and needy. Give me Your
wisdom and ability to recognize need. Help me
to do all I can to meet that need. Even though
I am young and my help may seem so little,
with You, O Lord, many big things can be done.
Give me Your favour. Establish the work of my
hands as I obey Your commands. Help me to
do it with a smile and may the poor feel loved
through me. Come and bless this day
as I look to You. Amen.

Memory Verse: *"I can do all things through
him who strengthens me."*
(Philippians 4:13, ESV)

PSALM 57:1-11

Dear God, please keep me faithful in helping and serving people. Show me the best way. Give me courage and kindness. Help me to use my money, time and talents to faithfully bless others and honour You. Lord, please help me to make the most of time, so I will be more productive in all things. I trust in You to help me get amazing things done ahead of time. May I live to be truthful and to be trusted in everything I do. Jesus, I want to live my life for You. Amen.

Memory Verse: *"It is more blessed to give than to receive."*
(Acts 20:35, ESV)

READ AND THINK ABOUT
PSALM 126

Dear Lord Jesus, thank You for being by my side night and day. You forever keep me in safety along life's way. Oh, how You fill my life with Your goodness! I have much fun and laughter. Many times we shout with joy. Our hearts are full because You have done so many great things for us. Thank You for: *(Name a great thing God has done for you.)* Lord, You are so gentle, good and kind. I'm so glad, Lord Jesus, for Your joy that we did find. Amen.

Memory Verse: *"Give thanks to the Lord, for he is good; his love endures forever."* (1 Chronicles 16:34, NIV)

READ AND THINK ABOUT

JAMES 1:1-12

Dear God, I call out to You and call upon Your Name, "Jesus." I want to love and freely obey Your commands. Jesus, I want to keep my eyes on You. I need the strength and power of the Holy Spirit to turn away from wrong. May I do what pleases You. In times of trouble, when I don't know what to do, help me to remember to call on You. Your wisdom is free. Thank You that You are more than willing to give answers of wisdom without finding any blame. So I put my trust in You and call on Jesus' name. Amen.

Memory Verse: *"If any of you lacks wisdom, he should ask God, who gives generously to all without finding fault, and it will be given to him."*
(James 1:5, NIV)

PSALM 34:1-14

Dear Heavenly Father, Almighty God, Your name is power. When I speak Your name, the name of Jesus, sin has no hold on me. All evil has to flee when I speak Your name. You name is power. I love Your name, "Jesus." May my lips forever praise Your Holy name. Your name is above every name and sets me free from all sin and shame. I give glory to Your precious name. O what a beautiful name, Lord Jesus. You are always the same. I'm so glad that You came for me, and that from sin You have set me free. Amen.

Memory Verse: *"...that at the name of Jesus every knee should bow, of those who are in heaven, and on earth, and under the earth."*
(Philippians 2:10, NASB)

READ AND THINK ABOUT
MATTHEW 27:27-56

Dear Lord Jesus, thank You for loving me.
Thank You for dying on the cross and shedding
Your blood for my sin. You took the
punishment that I deserve for sin so
that I now can be saved.
I am sorry for all the wrong things I have
done. I now turn away from sin. Please
forgive me of all my sin. Come into my heart
and life by Your Holy Spirit. Wash me and
make me pure. I surrender my life to You.
I want to belong to You. Amen.

Memory Verse: *"Believe in the Lord Jesus,
and you will be saved, you and your household."*
(Acts 16:31, ESV)

READ AND THINK ABOUT
MATTHEW 27:57-66

Dear God in Heaven, please forgive me of all
my sin. Please help me to turn away from all
that I know is wrong. Thank You for sending
Your Son, Jesus Christ, to take all my sin to
the cross where He bled and died for me.
Jesus, I believe that You died, were buried
and rose again from the grave. Please come
into my heart by Your Holy Spirit and be my
helper and true friend. Guide me into the
Way of Truth. I now receive Your forgiveness
of my sin and Your eternal life by faith
through Jesus Christ. Amen.

Memory Verse: *"Yet to all who received him,
to those who believed in his name, he gave
the right to become children of God."*
(John 1:12, NIV)

Jesus said to him: *"I am the way, and the truth, and the life. No one comes to the Father except through me."* (John 14:6, ESV)

MATTHEW 9:1-13

Dear God, You are always speaking to Your creation. I hear Your soft voice and Your tender call. Calling me to follow You. Calling me to believe in You. Calling me to trust in You. Calling me to receive all of You. Lord Jesus, I give my all to You. Come into my heart and life. Thank You for dying on the cross for my sin. Please forgive me for all of my sin. Come and walk beside me. Teach me the new way You want me to be. I am so glad I now belong to You, Jesus. Amen.

Memory Verse: *"Draw near to God, and he will draw near to you."*
(James 4:8, ESV)

MATTHEW 28

Dear Lord Jesus, please come into my heart by Your Holy Spirit. I am sorry for all the wrong things that I have done. Please forgive me and wash away all my sin. Thank You for dying on the cross for me. Thank You for shedding Your precious blood to cover all my sin and to free me from it. Holy Spirit, wash over me. Make my heart clean and pure. Then I'll feel most secure. Deliver me from evil stuff. Please help me not to be rough. Keep my ways gentle and good. Help me to love You the way I always should. Amen.

Memory Verse: *"You shall love the Lord Your God with all your heart and with all your soul and with all your mind."*
(Matthew 22:37, ESV)

ABOUT THE AUTHOR

Sandra grew up on a farm near Beausejour, Manitoba. She was the oldest of five children brought up in a Christian family.

At about age five, Sandra learned about Jesus and received Him into her life. At age nine, she had a powerful encounter with Jesus Christ and His power in the Holy Spirit.

Sandra received her post-secondary education in executive secretarial accounting in Winnipeg, Manitoba.

She liked sewing and quilting and has more lately pursued the fine arts through water colour and acrylic painting.

Sandra was much involved with her siblings, singing and performing special music at community gatherings, playing the accordion and piano, and later serving as a church organist for many years.

In 1961, Sandra married Herb, and shortly after they moved to Prince George, B.C. where they raised two sons.

She worked for many years in the School District Board Office.

After retiring, Sandra spent ten years developing children's ministry in a church plant for the Christian and Missionary Alliance; this time also included five years in after-school child evangelism in the schools in Prince George, B.C. Following that, together with her husband, Sandra spent about five years leading and hosting Alpha groups in Introduction to Christianity, Alpha Marriage and Alpha Pre-marriage.

Sandra served for six years on a church board of directors, also assisting in the purchase of the office and seminar building for the church plant.

In the fall of 2011, Sandra and her husband moved to Airdrie, Alberta, where they fully retired.

To find out more about Sandra,
check out her website at:

www.signetringrevelations.com